SMILE &
SUCCEED
FOR
Teens

A CRASH COURSE IN FACE-TO-FACE COMMUNICATION

Must-Know People Skills for Today's Wired World

Award-winning author of *Smile: Sell More with Amazing Customer Service*

KIRT MANECKE

SOLID
PRESS
LLC

D0032397

PRAISE FROM TEENS

"*Smile & Succeed for Teens* helped me realize that the way you put yourself into the world matters."
—NINA

"Now I know when to have my phone out and when not to."
—ISABELLE

"I found the book personally inspiring. I would not have known what to do and what not to do in an interview."
—JEREMIAH

"This book is very helpful as I often look down when I talk and I also have bad posture."
—BRANDON

"The book is valuable. For instance, I didn't really know there was a specific way to shake someone's hand."
—HANNAH

"My big brother and I want to start a dog-walking business. *Smile & Succeed for Teens* will really help us get started."
—CHASE

"This book helped me with eye contact, shaking hands, greeting people, and knowing what to wear for special occasions. I learned when to not be on my phone."
—GABI

"I found this book very helpful in using proper body language. I slouch a lot and now I know it isn't very respectful."
—NOLAN

"*Smile & Succeed for Teens* is useful to me because I am shy. I am a babysitter and I learned to smile and make eye contact. I love the pictures!"
—ISABELLA

"Now I know how to act in an interview."
—JAICIE

"The book is effective as I am not the best with eye contact."
—MATTHEW

"I like the tips and directions on smiling and how to shake hands."
—DEVON

"I use this book to prepare for an interview, get a job, learn how to speak to adults, and more."
—CHLOE

"I learned how *not* smiling can affect me. I am glad I read it."
—ANGELINA

Published by Solid Press, LLC. Inquiries about this book should be
addressed to the publisher: Solid Press, LLC, PO Box 145, Milford, MI 48381,
kirt@smilethebook.com or 248-685-0483.

Library of Congress Control Number: 2014904957

www.SmileforTeens.com

Legal Notice
Please note that much of this publication is based on personal experience that has
worked for the author. Your particular situation may not be exactly the same, and
you should adjust your use of the information accordingly. Nothing in this book
is meant to replace legal/professional advice. Please note that company websites,
while accurate at the time of publication, are subject to change. Websites printed in
this book are offered as a resource to you. These websites are not intended in any
way to be or imply an endorsement on the part of Solid Press, LLC, nor do we vouch
for the content of these sites for the life of this book.

**Special discounts for bulk purchases are available for educational, business,
fundraising or sales promotional use**. Special editions or book excerpts can also
be created to specifications. For details, please contact the Special Sales Department, Solid Press, LLC, PO Box 145, Milford, MI 48381, or kirt@smilethebook.com.

Summary: A quick, easy-to-read people and business skills handbook to
help middle school and high school age teens succeed in school, work, and life.

Book Design: Becky Terhune
Illustrations: Andre Jolicoeur

ISBN: 978-0-9850762-1-4

**A portion of the proceeds from the sale of this
book is donated to animal welfare.**

For young people working to
make our world a better place.

And to my parents, John and Betsy—
they lovingly taught me manners and
how to treat people with respect.
My business successes are in
large part due to them.

Also by Kirt Manecke:

Smile: Sell More with Amazing Customer Service

C☺NTENTS

CHAPTER THREE
KEEP THEM SMILING

CHAPTER FOUR
TREAT PEOPLE HOW YOU WANT TO BE TREATED

CHAPTER FIVE
SELL MORE WITH GREAT PEOPLE SKILLS

CHAPTER SIX
KEEP CUSTOMERS SMILING AFTER THE SALE
Create Happy Repeat Customers and Donors with Powerful

CHAPTER SEVEN
BE A ROCK STAR

ACKNOWLEDGMENTS

Writing a book is a team effort—I doubt many people could go it alone. Thanks from the bottom of my heart to all those who have contributed to this project: book publishing ace Becky Ferguson, English teacher and mother Sharon Hammer, teacher consultant Tammy Hansford, author Steve Fadie, teacher Rachel Ferguson, teacher Alicia Quintana, business coach Colleen Kilpatrick, sales expert Larry Betzler, bookstore buyer Pam Herman, librarian and grandmother Phyllis Brantingham, mother Tammy Duncan, product development expert Karen May, mother and customer service advocate Kathy Olak, mother of six Debi Lundwall, father and small business owner Peter Wottowa, father and author Joe Keller, customer service professional Amy Gresock, business leader Richard Lindhorst, book publishing expert Kim Walter, content editor Paula Manzanero, and the helpful trio of women at Main Street Art in downtown Milford, Michigan.

A huge thank-you to a superstar group of teens who made certain the content is valuable, relevant, and easy to read: Nick Keller, Terena Weitkamp, Ben Gottlieb, Sasha Dudock, Nova Rayner, and Curtis Schmitt.

A special thank-you to my parents, John and Betsy Manecke, and to my late uncle Gene Balogh, whose spirit and work have always been an inspiration to me.

Thank you to my wonderful editor Liz Parks for pulling this book together.

And finally thank you to all my friends and colleagues, including those not mentioned here, for their very valuable insight, patience, and support in this endeavor.

INTRODUCTION

Smiling can be a competitive advantage—it makes every person feel a little better, and every situation a little brighter.
—RICHARD BRANSON, FOUNDER OF VIRGIN GROUP, A LEADING INTERNATIONAL INVESTMENT GROUP

The Power of a Smile

When I was a teen I had a successful paper route, then a lawn-mowing service. Later I worked on the grounds crew at a golf course. **Good people skills** were key to my success.

You may wonder, exactly what are people skills? How do I learn them? The good news is, having good people skills is not that complicated. This book shows you exactly what you need to know.

In today's wired world, cell phones and other electronics, texting, and email are a reality. This makes having great people skills even more important. *Smile & Succeed for Teens* is based on my award-winning first book, *Smile: Sell More with Amazing*

Customer Service. Written for employers and employees, *Smile* received praise not only from the business community, but also from parents and educators. "Every teen in America needs to read this book!" one parent exclaimed. "It teaches important people skills kids need to succeed in their job and in life."

With input from a variety of teens, educators, and parents, I created a customized version of *Smile* just for you. Like my first book, the tips and techniques on the following pages are based on the same proven customer service and sales methods used by successful businesses all over the world. These techniques will help you make more friends and earn more money. In addition, I've added valuable information on finding and keeping a job, overcoming stress, and the benefits of volunteering.

Good people skills are essential for landing a job and succeeding in your career. Getting a job can be very challenging and frightening. *Smile & Succeed for Teens* can help you stand out during a job interview. It can help make you a superstar employee—the type companies jump through hoops to have on their team.

People skills are among the **top skills** businesses expect when interviewing and hiring. Employers everywhere are saying that young people lack the people skills critical to be successful at work.

Good people skills are also essential if you are starting your own business. Whether selling items from your garden at your local farmers' market, babysitting, lawn mowing, landscaping, tutoring, or working at a restaurant, you can *Smile & Succeed*!

Developing face-to-face communication skills is extremely important for young people. Personal relationships depend on them. So does success at school.

No other book presents valuable people skills customized for teens in such a short, simple format. You can read a chapter at a time and learn a new technique in just a few minutes. The contents can be read in any order. You can start today and have fun doing it!

THIS BOOK WILL HELP YOU:
- Develop people skills critical to success in a wired world
- Boost your self-esteem and confidence dealing with people
- Master people skills to create successful relationships with friends, parents, teachers, and customers
- Interview like a pro and get that job
- Develop customer service and sales skills to succeed on the job
- Be comfortable and confident selling and fundraising
- Become a successful young entrepreneur
- Enjoy volunteering and working more than you ever imagined

You'll learn how easy it can be to impress your friends and family, satisfy your customers, give back to your community as a volunteer, and create donors (people who donate to fundraisers and nonprofit organizations). The quick, easy tips will help you treat people with respect. You'll have more confidence at school and work. Your new people skills will make your customers smile and come back for more. You'll be comfortable selling and fundraising. You'll notice people coming back and talking positively about you.

Now get out there and smile!

HOW TO GET THE MOST OUT OF THIS BOOK

THIS BOOK IS A HANDBOOK. It's not a textbook. There won't be a quiz at the end (sigh of relief). If the ideas are new to you, you may want to take some time to digest and practice each chapter before moving on to the next. You can read straight through or consult the contents to decide which sections you want to read first. If this is your personal copy, don't be afraid to make notes and highlight important information.

The Top Ten People Skills will help you achieve success in school, work, and life. If you take away nothing else from this book, these 10 powerful techniques will help you create awesome relationships. Strong people skills produce a high degree of success in anything you do.

Take a few minutes or longer each week or month to review the entire book so the best practices become habit. Be sure to read all the chapters whether you are currently employed or not.

Some tips in this book may not seem important now, but they are. Whether or not you have a job, or will soon be working, the tips in this book will help you make more friends, and succeed in school and at work. Reviewing this book regularly will keep you sharp—and keep your friends, customers, and donors delighted!

1

THE TOP TEN PEOPLE SKILLS

How to Make Your Friends and Customers Smile

SMILE

Smile! Make it a good one. According to Malcolm Gladwell, author of *Blink*, first impressions occur instantly or within two seconds.

A smile can create a friend. It can create a customer for life. Smiling is one of the most important people skills.

A smile is powerful!

SMILE AND SAY HELLO

This may sound basic, but you'd be surprised how many people fail to greet others, whether family, friend, or customer, with a smile. When you meet someone

socially, focus on that person and greet him or her with a smile. When customers enter your workplace, greet each one promptly and politely.

HERE'S HOW

1. **Smile.** Make it a warm, genuine, heartfelt smile.
2. **Look people in the eye.**
3. **Say "Hello!"**
4. Speak in a warm, upbeat, and friendly manner. Be sincere.

Smile and the world smiles with you.

THE POWER OF A SMILE

When I owned a specialty retail store, I noticed that a teenage employee, Paul, was not smiling and greeting customers properly.

I pulled Paul aside and asked, "Why aren't you smiling and saying hello to customers when they walk in?" Paul responded, "They all hate me." I assured him he was wrong and asked why he felt that way. He said he just knew people didn't like him. I reminded him that we need to greet customers properly. I asked him to review our training, smile, and greet every customer, then see what happens.

That afternoon I observed Paul from a distance. He was greeting customers with a warm smile and a friendly "Hello." I spoke with Paul two days later. I asked how he was feeling. He exclaimed, "They all like me!" I replied, "Of course they do." From that day on Paul was our leading employee. That's the power of a smile!

WIRED TIP: ☺☺☺ All of these emoticons cannot equal a genuine, heartfelt smile from a real live person!

A smile is the curve that sets everything straight.
—PHYLLIS DILLER, COMEDIAN AND ACTRESS

Convey confidence and friendliness.

NOT GOOD

GOOD

MAKE GOOD EYE CONTACT

Eye contact is one of the best ways to make a positive impression. Good eye contact conveys respect, confidence, competence, honesty, and interest. It makes it easy for other people, including customers, to like and trust you. Looking people in the eye lets them know you are listening.

HERE'S HOW
1. Look the person in the eye.
2. Don't stare, but don't let your eyes wander either.
3. If you feel like you're staring, look at your customer's nose (no joke!).

Look at someone's nose when you're talking to them.

4. You can also blink, nod your head, and smile.

5. Maintain good eye contact throughout your conversation.

Good eye contact makes a powerful first impression.

Your parents will often want you to meet their friends. You may meet new customers at work. You may be nervous. You might feel hesitant at times because you don't know what to say. This is normal. Use each of these opportunities to practice good eye contact. The more you do it, the less anxiety you will feel.

The most positive conversations happen face-to-face.

 WIRED TIP: Electronic communication does not require eye contact. Face-to-face communication *demands* it.

Put the phone away.

TURN OFF THE ELECTRONICS

Your parents may bug you about turning off your phone, game, or computer. It may seem like they are being unreasonable, but they're not. If you are engrossed in an electronic device, you are not fully focused on the people around you. Cell phones, games, videos, texting, and surfing the Internet all keep you from practicing essential people skills.

Electronic devices are a huge part of our life. It's important to find a healthy way to manage their use. When used too often or inappropriately, **they can get in the way of your face-to-face social relationships.** And sometimes it's just plain rude. Give people your full attention.

NEVER use your cell phone or other digital device for personal use (texting, emails, phone calls, games) while at work. The only exception is if it's a tool required for your job.

ELECTRONIC ETIQUETTE

- Be careful. Whatever you text or post online lasts forever. Make sure it's positive and that you are always nice.
- **Photos last forever. Always ask a person's permission before taking or posting their picture.**
- If a personal email or text upsets you, don't respond right away. Wait at least 24 hours. This gives you time to think about it.
- Don't let your conversations be interrupted by text messages or cell phone calls. The exception is if it's your parents or a true emergency.
- It's okay to suggest that phones be turned off or left on vibrate when spending time with your friends.
- Don't text and drive. It's irresponsible, dangerous, and illegal in many places. If you need to contact someone in an emergency, pull into a parking lot.

Leave your electronic devices off or silenced:

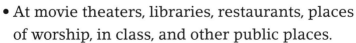

- At the dinner table.
- At important family functions.
- Anytime you are with people who want to have a face-to-face conversation with you.
- At movie theaters, libraries, restaurants, places of worship, in class, and other public places.
- At work (ALWAYS).

If you are not sure, just turn them off.

WIRED TIP: College admissions officers will review your social media and online profile before admitting you. Make sure your online reputation is professional and does not include questionable or inappropriate content or photos.

The person in front of you is more important than your phone.

—AMY CHAN, RELATIONSHIP COUNSELOR

SAY PLEASE AND THANK YOU

Good manners never go out of style. They are expected in all social and business situations.

SAY "PLEASE"

Say **"Please"** when you request something from your family, friends, or customers. For example, **"May I please borrow the car tonight?"** or **"Would you please unlock your gate so we can mow your backyard?"** Be sincere and genuine.

SAY "THANK YOU"

Say **"Thank you"** when someone does something nice for you. These two words cannot be overused when showing your appreciation.

Say "Thank you" even if your request is not granted. A "No" today does not mean a "No" forever. Whether or not your parents let you borrow the car (or whether your customer has made a purchase or donation or not), they took the time to consider your request. Using good manners might help you hear "Yes" the next time you ask.

When a customer leaves your business, thank them for coming in. Say "Thank you" in a warm and genuine manner. Or say "Thank you for coming in. I look forward to seeing you again."

Sometimes a telephone call, letter, or card is appropriate and meaningful. For example, when you receive a gift from your grandparents, don't text or email to thank them. Call and thank them on the phone or mail them a thank-you card or letter. **Do this within five days of receiving the gift.**

SAY "YOU'RE WELCOME"

When someone says "Thank you," answer with a smile and a polite **"You're welcome." Don't answer with "No problem," "Sure," or "Yep."** Always treat others with the utmost respect.

 WIRED TIP: "Please," "Thank you," and "You're welcome" are just as important over the phone and online as they are face-to-face.

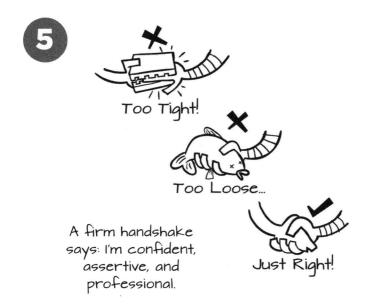

Too Tight!

Too Loose...

A firm handshake says: I'm confident, assertive, and professional.

Just Right!

SHAKE HANDS FIRMLY

A firm handshake creates a positive first impression. People form a lasting opinion of you from your handshake.

HERE'S HOW
1. Smile and look the person in the eye.
2. Put your right arm and hand out directly in front of you a few inches above waist level.
3. Grip the person's hand firmly. Say hello, introduce yourself, say their name, and shake their hand. Pump your right arm and hand together up and down two or three times for two to three seconds as you say,

"Hello, my name is _____. It's nice to meet you, __[their name]__."

Stand up when you shake hands. Never shake hands from a sitting position.

Students with high scoring handshakes are identified as the ones most likely to be hired.

You never get a second chance to make a good first impression.

—WILL ROGERS, AMERICAN HUMORIST AND ACTOR

Add meaning to your life— create good friendships.

INTRODUCE YOURSELF: MAKE A FRIEND

Friends are people you like and trust. It's important to remember the golden rule: **Treat people the way you'd like to be treated.**

Be nice, be polite, and smile. Don't be afraid to initiate a conversation with someone you would like to know. Make a friend!

HERE'S HOW

1. Greet people with a smile and a warm "Hello!"
2. Introduce yourself and shake hands. Say, "I'm
   __[your name]__ . It's nice to meet you."
3. Engage them in an initial short, friendly conversation
   and **pay attention.** Find out how they're doing: "It's
   nice to see you. How's your day going?" When appropriate, give a genuine compliment: "I really like that
   sweater."
4. Ask questions to get the other person talking about
   themselves. "Where do you go to school?" or "Where
   have you been on vacation?"
5. Listen carefully. Before long you'll probably find common interests and experiences you can talk about.
6. Once you have met someone, don't hesitate to speak
   to them the next time you see them. This is how good
   conversations and friendships are created.

When you are comfortable making new friends, it
will be easier to initiate conversations with people at
work. When you know how to make a friend, you will
know how to help people. Transitioning to the world of
work using your must-know people skills will be smooth
and successful.

**Friendship is
an undervalued
resource.**

WIRED TIP: For a list of helpful questions to ask when you first meet someone, go to www.SmileforTeens.com and click on "Free."

The only way to make a friend is to be one.
—RALPH WALDO EMERSON, AMERICAN ESSAYIST, LECTURER, AND POET

Stand out! Be a
good listener.

PAY ATTENTION

Listening is a must-know people skill. It builds trust, displays sincerity, and shows you care. Listening is essential for strong, positive relationships.

One of the most valuable skills you can learn from this book is to **PAY ATTENTION** to people.

HERE'S HOW
- Make good eye contact.
- Focus on the words they are saying.
- Ask questions to clarify when necessary.
- Engage in the conversation.
- Let people finish talking before you respond.

People often make the mistake of **not** listening carefully. They cut people off. They start to respond before someone is finished talking, leading to misunderstandings.

They don't ask clarifying questions. If it's a conflict or uncomfortable topic, good listening skills sometimes are forgotten. Paying attention to your friends, family, and customers leads to success in life and work.

AN UNHAPPY CUSTOMER

While dining at a restaurant I asked the server for their delicious garlic butter. The server forgot. I reminded him again. Something that could have helped him remember my request would have been to repeat it, saying, "I'll be right back with your garlic butter." When he finally came back to the table he brought olive oil. He missed an opportunity to create a good relationship with a customer. He also missed out on earning a better tip!

Multiple studies indicate that listening is a top skill needed for business success.

The word "listen" contains the same letters as "silent."

—ALFRED BRENDEL, AUSTRIAN PIANIST, POET, ARTIST, AND AUTHOR

Enthusiasm creates a positive, lasting impression.

BE ENTHUSIASTIC

Enthusiasm is contagious—just like a smile. Enthusiasm indicates interest, excitement, and passion.

Have you ever talked with people who seem totally uninterested, bored, or just plain dull? If so, you know the difference an upbeat attitude can make. Being with an enthusiastic person is energizing and engaging. It does not have to be loud or over the top. Be yourself. Be sincere. Don't try *too* hard.

In the world of work, be the person you'd want to be dealing with if *you* were in your customer's shoes. Your genuine enthusiasm, positive attitude, and interest in helping your customers will leave them delighted. Whether painting, babysitting, working at a bakery, landscaping, or working as a camp counselor, your enthusiasm will make their day!

The real secret of success is enthusiasm.
—WALTER CHRYSLER, FOUNDER OF THE CHRYSLER CORPORATION

ASK QUESTIONS

Good communication requires asking specific open-ended questions. Open-ended questions begin with **Who, What, When, Where, Why, or How.**

   Open-ended questions can't be answered with **"No."** This leaves the door open for more conversation.

What It Sounds Like: Closed-Ended Question
You: "Did you have fun on your trip to Florida?"
Friend: "Yes."

What It Sounds Like: Open-Ended Question
You: "What fun things did you do on your trip to Florida?"
Friend: "Our family went to Disney World. We swam in the ocean and went out to eat for lots of great seafood."

 WIRED TIP: When a complicated or personal issue is at stake, talk to the person face-to-face or by phone rather than texting.

Asking the right questions takes as much skill as giving the right answers.
—ROBERT HALF, FOUNDER OF ROBERT HALF INTERNATIONAL, RECRUITING AND PLACEMENT FIRM

Use positive body language to send the right message.

PRACTICE PROPER BODY LANGUAGE

Make sure you are aware of your body language. It says much more about you than you think. Send the message that you are confident, have a positive attitude, and act professionally.

HERE'S HOW
- **Smile.**
- **Look straight ahead and maintain good eye contact.**
- **Avoid looking down.**
- **Stand up straight.**
- **Look alert and approachable.** Leave your arms open at your sides (not crossed).
- **Respect people's personal space.** Recognize their comfort zone by noticing how far away from you they stand.

Respect yourself and others will respect you.
—CONFUCIUS, CHINESE PHILOSOPHER

2

GET
THAT
JOB

Use Your People Skills to Communicate Like a Pro

Landing a job
boosts your
confidence!

FIND THAT JOB

Finding a job can be challenging, especially when you are young. Many jobs are found through networking. Talk to teachers, family members, coaches, friends, parents, or anyone who can give you advice or contacts. (This is called networking.)

Your school counselor or career department can assist you. There are job-seeking websites. To access job-seeking websites visit www.SmileforTeens.com and click on "Free." Also look in your newspaper's classified section.

There are many types of jobs available. There may be jobs cleaning people's pools, babysitting, working construction, office work, working as a golf caddy, or mowing lawns. You may ask a neighbor if they would like to hire you to trim their hedges, grocery shop, or run errands for them.

Don't wait until July 4th to look for a seasonal or summer job. Use your time effectively. Start your job search as early as January. Many businesses have finished hiring by the beginning of the summer. Don't forget that many college students looking for summer jobs get out of school earlier than high school students. When you feel you are ready to work year-round and your parents agree, start looking immediately.

Your first job may not be your ideal job. It may be with a family friend or a business owned by people your parents or relatives know. Don't shy away from this. A first job is important. It will give you experience and valuable training. A successful first job will help you land your next job.

Once you know where you want to apply, follow the company's application instructions. Some require a resume and cover letter. Others require a simple application you can fill out in person or online. Online submission is one way companies screen applicants. Fill the application out completely and correctly with proper spelling.

Research the company before your interview. The company may first request a phone interview before inviting you in for a personal interview. Be upbeat, enthusiastic, and polite. Answer questions completely. Use your people skills to convince the inter-

Babysitting

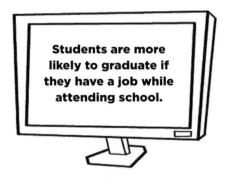

Students are more likely to graduate if they have a job while attending school.

viewer that you are the best candidate. They may bring you in for a second and third interview.

If the company is nearby, such as a retail store or restaurant, you can usually walk in and ask for a job application. Remember, this will be your first contact with this business. Make it spectacular. Visit in person and research them online first to learn everything you can about them. Dress neatly. You are creating your first impression. Smile and say: "I am very interested in working here. Could I please fill out an application?"

Be prepared to do more than just ask for an application. You may be asked additional questions on the spot. Make them smile—bring a copy of your resume and references.

If they say, "We are not hiring at the moment," ask, "Could I please fill out an application in case an opportunity comes up?" If you don't hear anything in a week or two, follow up by phone or in person and ask if anything has become available. This shows initiative and interest. Be persistent, not pushy.

TURN YOUR EXPERTISE INTO A JOB

In college I took a windsurfing course and learned all I could about the sport. During my sophomore year, I interviewed and landed a job at a windsurfing store. My knowledge and enthusiasm turned into a job! I worked on the sales floor and gave windsurfing lessons. Later I used this expertise to open my own business. You too can turn your expertise into a job!

A professional-looking cover letter and resume will impress employers.

 WIRED TIP: Prepare a neat looking cover letter and resume. Include points about your excellent people skills. See examples of a cover letter and resume at www.SmileforTeens.com and click on "Free."

Never, never, never give up.
—WINSTON CHURCHILL, FORMER PRIME MINISTER OF THE UK

With references in hand, you are one step closer to getting the job.

PUT TOGETHER POWERFUL REFERENCES

Good references are an important part of landing your dream job. Your references make you more credible in the job market. Plan ahead and gather your references before you need them.

Many employers rely on references to be certain people are of good character with a strong work ethic and good people skills. It's a big responsibility to get a job and be in someone's home or business. They may entrust you with the keys to their workplace. Always be professional.

Always ask for permission to use someone as a reference before listing them. Ask two or three non-relatives who know your skills and character.

HERE'S HOW

"Mr. Jones. I'm preparing my job search. Could I please include you in my list of references?" Then ask for the following information:

Name
Employer
Address
City, State Zip
Phone
Email

Add the following information:

Relationship to you
How long you've known this person

At the top of your reference sheet, put your name, complete address, and contact information. Then list each reference along with their complete information. Print these out on an 8½" x 11" sheet of white paper.

 **WIRED TIP:** To learn more about putting together references visit www.SmileforTeens.com and click on "Free."

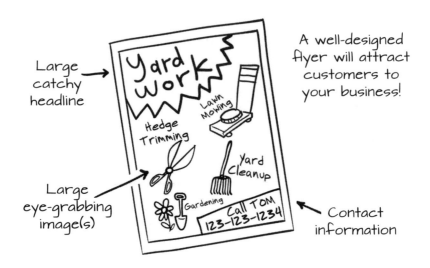

Large catchy headline

A well-designed flyer will attract customers to your business!

Large eye-grabbing image(s)

Contact information

CREATE YOUR OWN JOB: START WITH A FLYER

If you have your own business or want to start one, get the word out to potential customers. Create a flyer advertising your business. List your specific products or service, skills, and pricing.

Your flyer can be as simple as an 8½" x 11" sheet of paper. Use your computer to type the information or you can handwrite it if you or a friend has neat writing.

 WIRED TIP: To learn more about how to make a flyer for your business visit www.SmileforTeens.com and click on "Free."

Many a small thing has been made large by the right kind of advertising.

—MARK TWAIN, AMERICAN AUTHOR AND HUMORIST

Confident Smile

Dress for success

Fresh Breath

Up-to-date resume

with references

Tucked-in shirt

Impress your interviewer. Be prepared!

PREPARE FOR YOUR INTERVIEW

You want to make a good first impression.

HERE'S HOW
- Arrive at least 15 minutes early.
- Leave your cell phone and electronics off or on SILENT mode and out of sight.
- Look professional. Depending on the job, men should wear a dress shirt and dress pants and consider a sport coat and tie. Women should wear a blouse and slacks or skirt and consider a jacket.
- Avoid jeans, T-shirts, sneakers, hats, flip-flops, and visible body piercings. Cover up tattoos.

- Keep your hair neat and out of your face.
- Bring your resume and list of references.
- Be confident. Think positively. Smile and take a deep breath.

Before going for a job interview, review The Top Ten People Skills (pages 7–27) of this book. This will give you added confidence.

Prepare for the unexpected. As an employer, I've met many teens asking for job applications. If someone came in with must-know people skills and dressed appropriately, I would interview them on the spot!

TIP Make certain the voice mail greeting on your phone is professional. This will ensure you make a great first impression!

WIRED TIP: Before the interview, research the company online. Prepare a few questions to ask relevant to the job. For a list of suggested questions visit www.SmileforTeens.com and click on "Free."

BONUS WIRED TIP: Many employers will research your name online. If they find anything questionable, you may not get hired. Keep your online reputation clean! Your reputation is priceless.

You don't just luck into things as much as you'd like to think you do. You build step by step, whether it's friendships or opportunities.
—BARBARA BUSH, FORMER FIRST LADY

Show them
you want
the job!

INTERVIEW LIKE A PRO

The way you present yourself will determine if you get the job. If you develop great people skills, you stand a good chance of getting that job.

HERE'S HOW
- Be enthusiastic.
- Sit up straight.
- Listen attentively, smile, and make good eye contact.
- Don't chew gum.
- Be prepared to describe yourself in a few sentences.

Sit up straight, smile, make good eye contact, and listen.

- Common opening interview questions include "Tell me about yourself" and "Why do you want to work here?"
- Be prepared to explain why you are interested in the job. For example, "I'm interested in earning extra money this summer."
- Highlight skills and experiences you bring to the job. If you don't have previous experience tell them you want to learn.
- Answer questions honestly. Don't exaggerate or make things up. If you don't know the answer tell them what you *do* know and that you are interested in learning more.
- When the interviewer asks if you have any questions, ask about the job and its responsibilities. Save questions about days off, pay, vacation time, sick time, etc. for the end of the interview or the second interview.
- Thank the interviewer. Smile, make good eye contact, and shake hands firmly.
- Ask, "What's the next step?" or "When should I expect to hear from you?"

AFTER THE INTERVIEW

- **Mail a typed, formal thank-you letter to the interviewer as soon as you get home. Don't put this off.** It may seem like a small thing. It's not. This could be what gets you the job.

- **Also email a thank-you note to the interviewer the same day.** Why do both? Because you want the job and it is polite to do both.

- If you don't hear back after a week, call them to see if they've made a decision. Let them know you are still interested in the position.

Interview with all the grace and confidence you can muster.

Finally, supercharge your interview with your copy of *Smile & Succeed for Teens*. Hold it up and exclaim, "I read *Smile*. I have the must-know people skills that make me a good employee!"

 WIRED TIP: A thank-you text message or email is just the first step to show that you appreciate being interviewed. A typed thank-you letter shows that you really care and helps you stand out. It gives the employer one more reason to hire you. For an example of a thank-you letter visit www.SmileforTeens.com and click on "Free."

 BONUS WIRED TIP: It's normal to be nervous before, during, and after an interview. Preparing for the interview ahead of time will help ease your fears. Ask a friend or family member to hold a practice interview. For a list of questions visit www.SmileforTeens.com and click on "Free."

KEEP YOUR JOB

Once you land a job you will want to work hard to keep it.

HERE'S HOW

> The most common mistake new employees make is not dressing professionally.

- Follow directions
- Communicate clearly
- Be on time
- Be enthusiastic
- Practice self-control
- Take responsibility for assigned tasks
- Be able to work without supervision
- Be respectful
- Accept instruction eagerly

Why do most young people lose a job?
- Being late or being absent
- Not making an effort to get along with others
- Slow to learn good work habits

Remember to always be grateful that you have a job. Satisfied employers are good references for future jobs.

Excellence is not a skill. It is an attitude.
—RALPH MARSTON, FORMER PROFESSIONAL
FOOTBALL PLAYER

OVERCOME STRESS

Dealing with stress is like getting ready for a big football game or presentation. Prepare, eat right, and get enough sleep to be your best.

Too much stress can affect your health and the way you feel about life. It can affect your school and job performance. The good news is there are easy ways to deal with stress.

Remember the importance of smiles, not just directed at others, but directed at ourselves as well. Try it. Make a pouty, sad face, scrunch up your mouth so the corners turn down, and try to say something positive to yourself. Hard, isn't it?

Now smile and say the same thing. The smile makes your body more receptive to what you are saying. It does the same thing when you smile at someone else.

49% of teens report having difficulty sleeping due to stress.

Although stress is common in all our lives, a certain amount of stress motivates us to get things done.

Overcome stress to be your best in life and at work.

HERE'S HOW

- Think positively about yourself and others. Smile at your friends, family, classmates, teachers, customers, and coworkers. Too often we say or think negative things that are not true. ("I can't do this," "I'm lousy at that," "I'm not a good person," "I'm not attractive enough"). Don't let the negative take over. Replace negative thoughts with positive thoughts about yourself.
- Exercise or play sports. Physical activity relieves stress. Walk your dog. Run. Do yoga.
- Read.
- Take up a new hobby.
- Help others. Volunteer.
- Meditate.
- Focus on deep breathing. Take in as much air as you can—all the way down to your mid-section. Exhale and release the air slowly and evenly. It's relaxing. Feel that stress melt away.
- Surround yourself with positive people.

- Find the humor in situations and in life.
- Forgive and forget.
- Take time to talk regularly with your family and friends about things going on in your life.
- Recognize the difference between things you can do something about and things you can't. Act on the ones you can change. Learn to accept the ones you cannot.
- Break tasks into smaller chunks that will be easier to complete.
- Ask for help when needed.

You may be able to turn some of these techniques into a job. A good friend of mine loves golf. He joined the golf team in high school and got a job at the golf course as a caddy. The takeaway? Expand on your hobbies and sports and turn your passion into a job.

 **WIRED TIP:** For tips to overcome stress at home and at school visit www.SmileforTeens.com and click on "Free."

Whether you think you can, or you think you can't—you're right.
—HENRY FORD, AMERICAN INDUSTRIALIST, FOUNDER OF THE FORD MOTOR COMPANY

3

KEEP THEM SMILING

More Top People Skills for Life, Work, and Volunteering

APOLOGIZE AND MEAN IT

No matter how good your people skills are, sometimes mistakes happen. Knowing when and how to apologize is an important social skill. A proper apology builds and maintains healthy relationships.

An apology doesn't change what happened, but it does show that a person has accepted responsibility for their actions. It's not always easy, but it's important. Make sure you do it right.

HERE'S HOW

1. Say, "I'm sorry for _____." (Be specific about what you are sorry for.)
2. You may be used to simply saying "sorry" or "sorry about that," but that's not enough.
3. Be sincere. Say it like you mean it.
4. Wait for a response.

Examples

- "I'm sorry I spoke badly about you behind your back. It won't happen again."
- "I'm sorry I forgot your coffee. Here's a free dessert for you."

These words can be very difficult to say, but they make all the difference in the world.

WIRED TIP: Delivering an apology over the Internet is okay, but the most effective apology is always delivered in person. For more ways to apologize visit www.SmileforTeens.com and click on "Free."

An apology is the superglue of life. It can repair just about anything.
—LYNN JOHNSTON, CANADIAN CARTOONIST, *FOR BETTER OR FOR WORSE*

Hello Tammy!
Hi Josh!
Hey Steve!

People are impressed when you remember their name!

CALL PEOPLE BY NAME

One of the best ways to make a great impression on a person is to remember his or her name and use it. People love hearing their name!

HERE'S HOW
1. Smile.
2. Look them in the eye.
3. Enthusiastically say, "Hello, __[their name]__ ."

Don't assume it's all right to call adults by their first name unless they are close friends or family members who have given you permission to do so. To address adults, use Mr., Mrs. (married woman), Ms. (when you are not sure if a woman is married or not), Professor, or Dr., along with their last name.

Pronounce names correctly. If you are not positive how a name is pronounced, don't be afraid to ask.

If you're working with a customer and you don't know his or her name, try this:

HERE'S HOW

1. "Hello. My name is _____."

2. If they don't tell you their name in return, feel free to ask for it by saying, "And you are?"

 WIRED TIP: Whether online or handwritten, people notice when their name is misspelled. Spell names correctly. Check online for proper spelling.

A person's name is to that person the sweetest and most important sound in any language.
—DALE CARNEGIE, AUTHOR OF *HOW TO WIN FRIENDS AND INFLUENCE PEOPLE*

BE PREPARED: THE SIX P's

"Proper Preparation Prevents Pathetically Poor Performance." If you follow this advice for everything you do in life, you'll be way ahead of the pack.

Proper preparation means **having everything you need ready ahead of time.** Being prepared gives you confidence and builds the confidence of others in you.

HERE'S HOW
- Prepare for the unexpected.
- Complete homework at home.
- Assemble everything you need for the next day *before* you go to bed: backpack, clothes, homework, lunch, and school supplies.
- Winging it rarely works.

Things *seem* to work easily for some teens. But you may not realize how much preparation goes into "being lucky." Graham is in tenth grade. He read my first book, mastered the people skills, landed a job, and put

When you are well prepared, people feel you know your stuff.

the techniques to work. The owners work around Graham's schedule, and he is the only employee invited to work whenever he's available. He may seem lucky, but he properly prepared and followed it up with hard work. This is why things "look easy" for him. The good news is the same can happen for you!

Give me six hours to chop down a tree, and I will spend the first four hours sharpening the axe.
—ABRAHAM LINCOLN, 16ᵀᴴ PRESIDENT OF THE UNITED STATES

Make a great
first impression!

DRESS FOR SUCCESS

People form an opinion of you within the first few seconds of meeting you. And yes, they do judge a book by its cover.

Many businesses have dress codes. Some are very casual. Others are more businesslike. Some provide a uniform. If they don't tell you what the dress code is, be sure to ask.

If you are not sure if what you are wearing fits the dress code, it's safer to dress more businesslike. Your first job is the best place to show how professional you can be.

Keep your clothes, including uniforms, clean and neat. Wash them regularly. Iron if necessary. Keep your shoes clean and in good condition. Make sure you know if your dress code allows for jewelry or accessories. A word of caution about visible tattoos and body piercings: some employers may have dress codes regarding these.

Pay attention to your grooming. In all situations a neatly groomed, smartly dressed look is best. Make sure you smell good! Shower or bathe daily. Avoid too much perfume or cologne—some people are very sensitive to smells. Keep your nails clean and hair neat. Have breath mints on hand to keep your breath smelling fresh!

 WIRED TIP: To save money on work clothes that may not become part of your personal wardrobe, search online for consignment shops or stores such as a Salvation Army or Goodwill near you.

Before anything else, preparation is the key to success.
—ALEXANDER GRAHAM BELL, INVENTOR OF THE TELEPHONE

KEEP IT PROFESSIONAL

The last thing a customer wants to hear is an employee complaining about the job or talking about his or her personal life.

You should always be professional. Everything you say and do reflects on your place of employment.

HERE'S HOW
- Stay focused on the tasks you've been assigned. Save personal matters until you leave work.
- Keep conversations in the workplace positive and businesslike.
- Don't complain. Don't have personal conversations with coworkers in front of customers.

- Be aware that customers can hear you even if you are not face-to-face with them. Think: dressing rooms, drive-through windows, waiting rooms, front desks, and stockrooms.
- Don't comment negatively about your employer or the business.
- Go above and beyond when business is slow. Ask your manager what you can do to help.
- Give yourself the edge up at work. Take the initiative to complete extra assignments.

 WIRED TIP: Leave your electronics off and out of sight whether there are customers in your business or not. Talking or texting on your cell phone creates a negative first impression for a customer.

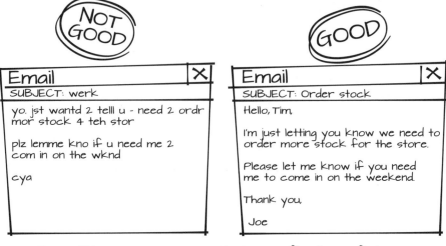

Everything you say or write is a reflection of YOU.

MASTER ELECTRONIC ETIQUETTE

Presentation is everything—including texting, sending emails, and using social media.

HERE'S HOW

- Use **proper English.** Use **proper grammar and punctuation.**
- Use **complete sentences.**
- Spell words out completely. Never use casual acronyms like "TY" (thank you).
- Include a **suitable and specific subject line.**
- Include a **proper salutation** (greeting) and **closing.**
- **Say please and thank you.**
- **Proofread, spell-check, and reread every message you write before sending or posting.**

An email is a professional means of communication. Treat it as such. Whether employed by someone else or if you work for yourself, these little things, done right, will help separate you from the pack.

Don't take shortcuts!

If you are using a text to communicate with work-related individuals, it should be written properly as well. **Don't shorten your message just because it's a text and you are trying to do less typing.** A text that is not properly written can be viewed as disrespectful and rude.

A properly written email is part of your professional reputation.

 WIRED TIP: Shouting is never professional. Avoid "ALL CAPS."

Product and service knowledge makes you an expert.

LEARN YOUR BUSINESS

Learn everything you can about the business you work for and your specific job responsibilities. For example, know business hours, pricing, and procedures by heart. The training provided to you may or may not be enough. You may need to take the initiative to learn more on your own. Your goal is to become an exemplary employee who is able to address customer concerns and questions with confidence. This will ensure that your customers are pleased.

The staff at my business had exceptional people skills and was very knowledgeable about our products. We also learned everything we could about competing businesses. Knowing the competition helped us better serve our customers and increased our sales.

Knowledge is power.
—SIR FRANCIS BACON, ENGLISH PHILOSOPHER, STATESMAN AND AUTHOR

MAKE IT EASY FOR CUSTOMERS TO DO BUSINESS WITH YOU

When a customer makes a reasonable request, reply with, **"Yes, I'd be happy to do that!"** or **"I'm happy to check on that for you!"**

Always listen to the customer, client, or patient. Do your best to help them and fulfill their request. Assume they wouldn't be asking if the issue wasn't important to them.

Never say "I can't." Never say "That's our policy" as a reason for denying a request.

WHAT IT SOUNDS LIKE

Customer: "Can I get the supreme pizza without onions?"
You: "I'll be happy to check and see if they can leave them off."
Customer: "Thank you!"
You: "You are welcome."

Customer: "We are having company over Thursday evening. I know you usually don't mow our lawn until Friday. Is there any way you could mow it Thursday instead so it looks nice for our party?"
You: "Yes, I'll be happy to do that."
Customer: "Thank you very much."
You: "You are welcome."

Customer: "I forgot my new health insurance card. Do I need it?"

You: "I'm sorry. Since it's new insurance we will need it."

Customer: "I understand. I'll go get it."

You: "Thank you."

If you are unable to help the customer or do not have the authority to address their issue, locate someone who does. If no one is available to help you, tell the customer that you or your supervisor will get back to them with an answer. Write down their name, phone number, and the date. Give this note to your supervisor. Go the extra mile by following up with your supervisor on the outcome.

Americans tell an average of 15 other people about a good customer service experience.

TIP Going the extra mile is a powerful way to surprise and delight your employer and your customers. It builds loyalty and respect for you and the business you work for!

Instead of saying no, figure out a way to say yes!
—KIRT MANECKE, AUTHOR OF THIS BOOK

Make great follow-up
skills a habit!

FOLLOW UP

Follow-up is key to providing amazing customer service and making sales. Always follow up promptly with customers.

PHONE

Return phone calls right away—at least by the end of the business day—within 24 hours at the latest. If the customer does not answer, leave a message that includes your name, the name and phone number of your company, and your reason for calling.

Do not allow an unanswered message to remain on your voice mail for more than 24 hours.

EMAIL

Respond to email inquiries from customers as soon as possible—at least by the end of the business day—within 24 hours at the latest.

SOCIAL MEDIA

Social media requires an even faster response. Research shows that 32% of customers expect a response within 30 minutes. 42% expect a response within 60 minutes.

IN PERSON

Anytime a customer is waiting for a product or service, you need to follow up with them regularly. Keep them updated on such things as: your arrival time, the status of their appointment, or of any delays.

These are just a few examples:
- In restaurants, inform customers every fifteen minutes if food orders are backed up.
- Inform customers on the status of their appointment in waiting rooms on a consistent basis.
- If the customer is waiting off-site at home or somewhere else, consistent updates are still very important. For example, if they are waiting for car repairs, let your customer know when they can expect to hear from you. Follow through with regular updates as needed.

Don't leave customers wondering what's going on, feeling disrespected, or ignored.

TIP In all situations do what you say you're going to do. Many businesses neglect this simple rule and end up losing customers. When you tell someone you'll "call them right back" or "get right back to them," do it! Your customers will know they can count on you.

Worry about being better; bigger will take care of itself. Think one customer at a time and take care of each one the best way you can.
—GARY COMER, FOUNDER OF LAND'S END

4

TREAT PEOPLE HOW YOU WANT TO BE TREATED

More Top People Skills and Customer Service Techniques

Acknowledge new customers promptly and politely.

ACKNOWLEDGE NEW CUSTOMERS—EVEN WHEN YOU'RE BUSY

Have you ever walked into a business and been ignored? There are countless stories of people left waiting: in restaurants, in retail stores, in hotels, in medical/dental facilities. After failing to be acknowledged, they simply leave and spend their money elsewhere. Don't let this happen to you!

Immediately acknowledge new customers.

HERE'S HOW

1. Smile.

2. Greet them with a warm **"Hello!"**

3. Look them in the eye and say, **"I'll be right with you"** or **"I'll be with you in a few minutes, as soon as I finish up with my customer."**

When you *do* get to that customer, say, **"Thank you so much for waiting! What exactly can I help you with today?"**

If you know you're going to be tied up for a while, say, **"Hello, I'm with a customer. Let me get someone to assist you."** Excuse yourself from your current customer for a moment and find someone to help the new customer.

Seventy percent of small business customers will make their purchases at another shop if they feel the sales staff doesn't care.

Everyone has an invisible sign hanging from their neck saying, "Make me feel important." Never forget this message when working with people.
—MARY KAY ASH, FOUNDER OF MARY KAY COSMETICS, INC.

How much longer do you think she'll wait?

Tap Tap Tap

HELP CUSTOMERS PROMPTLY

Most people hate to wait, whether at the doctor's office, in line at the bank, at home waiting for service, or for someone to complete a transaction over the phone.

Always keep an eye out for customers who are waiting for assistance. If they haven't been assisted, **jump in and see how you can help.**

If it turns out the customer is already being taken care of, find out who's helping

Two-thirds of dissatisfied customers have walked out of a store in the past year because of poor customer service.

them. Ask your fellow employees if there's anything you can do to assist them in making the transaction go faster. Often, there is!

 WIRED TIP: Even a short wait can seem like an eternity in our speedy wired world. It's especially important that customers know you are doing your best to keep wait times short.

Good afternoon.
Montgomery Inn.
This is Alex.
How may I help you?

Your smile
"shines through"
the phone line!

ANSWER THE PHONE WITH A SMILE

You already know the importance of making a great first impression. It's equally important over the phone. When you answer the phone at work, you're the first contact the customer has with your business. It's critical that you make a great impression.

How do you make a great impression over the phone? It's simple—**smile as you answer the phone.**

You may not realize it, but a smile totally changes the tone of your voice. Try it out! Your happy, smiling voice will delight your customers and your family and friends as well. Create a positive impression of yourself and the business.

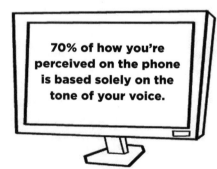

70% of how you're perceived on the phone is based solely on the tone of your voice.

HERE'S HOW

1. Smile.

2. Say, "Good morning [or afternoon or evening]!"
   Be sure to speak clearly.

3. State the complete name of your business.

4. Say: "This is ___[your name]___ . How may I help you?"

Be upbeat, warm, inviting, and genuine.

Here are a few other pointers for amazing customer service over the phone:

1. Try to answer the phone within two rings and definitely within three.

2. Call the customer by name when possible.

3. Always thank the customer for calling.

TIP If you have trouble hearing or understanding the person you are talking to, say, "I'm sorry. I did not understand that. Would you please repeat it?"

 WIRED TIP: Test your "phone" smile on a friend. Smile the next time you answer the phone. For more tips on using the phone visit www.SmileforTeens.com and click on "Free."

"Small stuff" matters. A lot!

—TOM PETERS, AUTHOR OF *THE LITTLE BIG THINGS* AND *IN SEARCH OF EXCELLENCE*

HOLD, PLEASE: ASK PERMISSION FIRST

Another opportunity to make customers smile is when you need to put someone on hold.

HERE'S HOW

Before you place your customer on hold:

1. Ask for permission.
2. Let them know how long they can expect to wait.
3. Thank them for holding.

If you think it might be a long wait, ask if they'd prefer you call them back. If so, be sure you write down their name and phone number.

WHAT IT SOUNDS LIKE

You: "May I please place you on hold for two minutes while I find the answer for you?"
Customer: "Certainly."
You: "Thank you. I'll be right back with your answer."
When you return to the phone, say, **"Thank you for holding."**

If the hold time becomes longer than expected, simply pick up the phone and inform them:
You: "I'm sorry. I told you I'd have an answer in two minutes. It's actually going to take me a few more minutes. May I please put you back on hold, or would

you prefer that I take your number and call you back when I have the answer?"

Finally, if your business is busy, like a pizza place on a Friday night, be careful not to leave out any part of the introduction. Proper phone etiquette is important even when you are busy.

"Good evening, Joe's Pizza. This is Susan speaking. May I please put you on hold?" Wait for them to answer before you place them on hold.

Don't just answer the phone with, "Joe's Pizza. Please hold."

Even though people may not like being put on hold, most don't mind waiting if you ask properly and politely. Chances are you'll return to a happy customer.

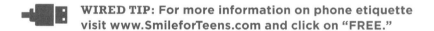 **WIRED TIP:** For more information on phone etiquette visit www.SmileforTeens.com and click on "FREE."

No matter how busy you are, you must take time to make the other person feel important.
—MARY KAY ASH, FOUNDER OF MARY KAY COSMETICS, INC.

Seal the deal with careful counting!

GIVE CHANGE CAREFULLY

Giving change should be done with good eye contact and a smile. **It's part of the entire customer experience.**

When you give a customer change, first **make eye contact and smile.** Then **present the change so the customer can easily handle it and put it in their wallet or purse.**

HERE'S HOW

1. Place the coins in their hand first.
2. Then give them the bills.
3. Don't hand a customer receipts, dollar bills, and coins all heaped together. This makes it hard for the customer to put everything away.

A friend of mine was at a national fast food chain drive-through. The cashier handed her the dollar bills, then "launched" the coins at her. The coins landed underneath her car. Don't be this cashier!

COUNT CHANGE CAREFULLY

It's important to count the change back to your customer so you *both* know you gave the correct amount. You might be held accountable for any shortages.

WHAT IT SOUNDS LIKE

You: "Your change is $12.67—that's 50, 60, and 67 cents *(as you place the two quarters, dime, nickel, and two pennies in their hand)*, and 10, 11, and 12 *(as you place the ten and two dollar bills in their hand)*."

Make eye contact and smile when you're done counting out the change. Finish by saying "**Thank you!**"

TIP Keeping an organized cash drawer is professional. It will help you make change quickly.
• Keep bills facing in the same direction and facing up.
• Place bills and coins in their proper location.

5

SELL MORE WITH GREAT PEOPLE SKILLS

More Secrets to Successful Selling and Fundraising

"JUST LOOKING": LET THEM BROWSE AND SHOP

When someone tells you they're "Just looking," let them browse. Don't intimidate them by walking toward them and trying to initiate an immediate sale.

Tell your customer you'll be available if and when they need help. You can set up the expectation that you'll be back by saying, **"Great! My name is _____. I'll check back with you in a bit to see if you have any questions."** This makes it easy to go back and talk to them again.

As your customer continues to look around, take care not to hover. Some people genuinely want to browse on their own. Check in on them from a distance from time to time.

Watch for signs that they may need some help:
- Making long eye contact with you
- Looking around for someone to help them
- Spending a long time checking out one product or service

If a coworker has already asked a customer if they need help and they've said, "Just looking," don't ask them again. Approach them if you see a sign that they're looking for help.

NEVER ASK "CAN I HELP YOU?"

When you ask "Can I help you?" it's too easy for customers to say "No" and end the interaction.

Instead, ask your customer an **open-ended question,** such as:

"How can I help you?"

"What can I help you with today?"

"What exactly are you looking for today?"

Use open-ended questions in the workplace to uncover your customer's needs and wants. Pay attention to their responses.

WHAT IT SOUNDS LIKE

Salesperson: "What can I help you with today?"

Customer: "I'm looking for a new chainsaw for my wife to replace her current chainsaw."

Salesperson: "What is wrong with her current chainsaw?"

Customer: "The chainsaw she has works fine. It's just too heavy for her to carry for a long time."

Salesperson: "The Stihl electric chainsaw is lighter weight than a gas chainsaw. It'll be light enough for your wife to carry all day long. How does that sound?"

Customer: "It sounds perfect!"

The best salespeople are more naturally curious than less successful salespeople.

Nobody cares how much you know, until they know how much you care.
—THEODORE ROOSEVELT, 26TH PRESIDENT OF THE UNITED STATES

Pointing confuses customers. Walking your customer to the proper products helps you sell more!

DON'T POINT— WALK AND SHOW

If a customer asks you where something is located, don't point to the location or just tell them the aisle number.

Instead, **walk the customer to the exact location and show them the exact product or service they're looking for.**

DON'T BE THIS GUY

I was in a major hardware chain store near my hometown recently.

I approached a clerk and said, "Hello." He grunted. I asked him if they carried wire. He said, "Yeah."

I asked him where it was. He pointed at a huge maze of aisles. I asked him which aisle it was in.

He grunted again, "Aisle 5." **Don't be this guy!**

TIP Walking your customer to their destination is a **"must-do"** in retail, and a **"should-do"** whenever possible in other jobs.

It is estimated that $83 billion is lost by U.S. businesses every year because of poor customer service.

Be as helpful as you can.

WHEN YOU DON'T KNOW THE ANSWER, ASK

Sometimes you will be asked questions that you can't answer. **Never say, "I don't know" without offering to find the answer.**

Be honest and say, **"That's a great question. I don't know the answer, but I'll find someone who does so they can help you."**

Or, **"I'm not sure, but I'll go find out and be right back."**

Finding answers to customers' questions are opportunities for you to learn more about the business you work for or your own business. The more you know, the more confident you become.

Knowledge is power!

Your must-know people skills are
traits of an effective salesperson.

SELL WITH CONFIDENCE

It's normal to have some fear when you start a new job. If your job involves selling, you may be even more uncomfortable. You might feel like you are bothering the customer.

Think of selling as **helping the customer buy what they need.** After all, if they didn't need your product or service, they wouldn't have come to your workplace.

When you're shopping for something you need, think of how grateful you are to find someone who's both helpful and knowledgeable—that's a good salesperson!

By helping customers buy what they need, you are providing good customer service. Maybe you've compared features and warranties. Perhaps you've looked at brands and gone over pricing. You've done your homework. Be confident. You have the skills of an effective employee.

 **WIRED TIP:** For selling tips visit www.SmileforTeens.com and click on "Free."

The only thing we have to fear is fear itself.
—FRANKLIN DELANO ROOSEVELT, 32ND PRESIDENT OF THE UNITED STATES

If you don't ask your customer for the sale, the answer is always no.

ASK FOR THE SALE—THEN STOP TALKING

Once you've helped your customer and they are ready to buy, ask for the sale. Then be quiet. Don't utter a sound.

WHAT IT SOUNDS LIKE: ASK FOR THE SALE
You: "Would you like to buy it?"

Then be quiet.

Customer: *(Silence for a few seconds as he or she thinks about it…)* "What types of payment do you accept?"
You: "We accept credit cards, debit cards, cash, or check. How would you like to pay?"

Then BE QUIET, even if it means there's silence for 30 seconds or more. This rule applies whether you're speaking in person or on the phone. If you stay quiet, the customer is much more likely to answer with a "Yes!"

Customer: "I'll pay by credit card. Here's my Visa."

We usually say too much. It makes us less persuasive.
—KATYA ANDRESEN, NONPROFIT MARKETING EXPERT AND AUTHOR OF *ROBIN HOOD MARKETING*

The right promotion will bring customers to you.

PROMOTE YOUR BUSINESS OR EVENT

When I was in school I started a lawn service. I went door to door around our neighborhood and handed out flyers. I asked people if they would like their lawns mowed. Many said, "Yes!"

One way to promote your business or event is to distribute a flyer. Check with your parents first to see if they support the idea of handing out flyers in your neighborhood. Ask them to distribute them to people they know who might be interested. You also can use social media and create a website to promote your business.

Think about who your potential customers are. Avoid getting frustrated if you don't see results right away from your promotion. It takes time to get results. Get your information into the hands of people most likely to use your product or service. For example, if you are promoting your babysitting business, target people who have children. And remember that by providing top-notch work, word of mouth will bring you even more business.

 WIRED TIP: To learn more about how to promote your business or event visit www.SmileforTeens.com and click on "Free."

Marketing is a contest for people's attention.
—SETH GODIN, BESTSELLING AUTHOR AND MARKETER

6

KEEP CUSTOMERS SMILING AFTER THE SALE

Create Happy Repeat Customers and Donors with Powerful People Skills

HANDLE RETURNS GRACIOUSLY

Returns are a part of doing business. When a customer requests a refund, whether canceling a service or returning a product, use your must-know people skills. **Be upbeat, cheerful, and helpful. Tell the customer you're sorry things didn't work out and that you're happy to help.**

Never take a return personally. Have you ever returned an item or canceled a service and the person you dealt with seemed annoyed? Don't be this person!

Your customer may feel awkward about returning the item or canceling the service. It's your job to set them at ease.

A KID AND HIS PUNCHING BAG

When I was 10 years old, I had a punching bag that leaked. I sent it back and wrote a letter to the company explaining my problem. I really didn't expect to hear anything back, but two weeks later a package arrived. To my surprise and delight, it contained a nice letter from the company—and a brand-new punching bag.

The story might have ended there, but the new bag also leaked. I sent it back again, this time really expecting the cold shoulder. To my shock and amazement, the company sent me another nice letter along with another replacement punching bag—this time, their top-of-the-line model. This bag did not leak, and I went on to use it happily for many years.

Needless to say, I was thrilled by my experience with the company (picture me as a boy smiling from ear to ear). I've been a satisfied customer ever since. This was such a good experience for me that this is the way I handle customer service in my business. This company not only won me back with their amazing customer service, they created a customer for life.

HERE'S HOW

1. Smile graciously. Be kind and understanding.
2. Say: **"I'm sorry things didn't work out. I'll be happy to assist you."**

It takes 12 positive customer service experiences at a business to make up for one negative one.

3. Complete the transaction with efficiency, friendliness, and respect.
4. Say: "I look forward to helping you in the future. Thank you."

REMEMBER A return is an opportunity to leave the customer with a positive impression. Handling returns kindly with a genuine smile creates lifelong customers.

Customer service is just a day-in, day-out, ongoing, never-ending, unremitting, persevering, and compassionate type of activity.
—LEON GORMAN, CEO OF L.L. BEAN

Provide great customer service and your customers will sing your praises.

TURN COMPLAINERS INTO ADVOCATES

Think of customer complaints as opportunities. An unhappy customer may be complaining about:

- The service or quality of an item
- Poor customer service

When you handle a complaint promptly and effectively, an unhappy customer can become a valued customer—one who spreads the word about you and your business. Handling complaints properly is an important part of delivering

Satisfied customers who have problems resolved will tell five people about their good experience.

great customer service and selling more. It's important to keep complaints in perspective. They should not be taken personally, even though they may feel personal.

HERE'S HOW

1. **Listen attentively and let the customer talk.** Sometimes all the customer needs is to vent and have someone listen.
2. **Look the customer in the eye and say, "I'm sorry." Don't say, "Sorry" or "Sorry about that"**—it doesn't sound sincere. **Be genuine.**
3. **Thank the customer for bringing the problem to your attention.**
4. Assure them you'll look into it immediately and resolve the issue so it doesn't happen again.
5. **If you are not able to solve the customer's issue, locate your supervisor for the appropriate solution.**

DID YOU KNOW?

80% of companies *think* they're providing superior service. Customers say only 8% are hitting the mark.

When written in Chinese, the word "crisis" is composed of two characters. One represents danger, and the other represents opportunity.
—JOHN F. KENNEDY, 35TH PRESIDENT OF THE UNITED STATES

7

BE A
ROCK
STAR

**Use Your Expertise
and People Skills to
Change the World**

Your skills can help solve our
world's most pressing problems.

MAKE YOUR LIFE EXTRAORDINARY: MAKE A DIFFERENCE

Volunteer and change the world. Watching the beautiful forests and fields around my childhood home turn into subdivisions and office buildings prompted my interest in volunteering. The business community did massive amounts of advertising to sell new homes and office space. I wondered where the conservation groups were. Why weren't they getting the word out to preserve some of this land?

As it turns out, they lacked the necessary skills and funds. I recognized a huge need for these groups to get the word out and raise funds to create change. I felt a need to help them do this. I read everything I could to educate myself about the issues. I joined organizations and volunteered. Eventually these experiences led to a fundraising job with a nonprofit land conservancy preserving land in northern Michigan. A nonprofit organization, also referred to as a charity, is created with the goal of doing good and helping the public. If you are good at sales, fundraising, or getting the word out, nonprofits need your help.

A childhood experience led to my involvement with nonprofit organizations. This participation adds purpose to my life. Using my sales experience, I raise funds for causes close to my heart. Working or volunteering for a cause close to your heart can be just as gratifying for you.

To close your eyes will not ease another's pain.
—CHINESE PROVERB

You are the person many causes are waiting for.

ROCK STARS WANTED

Nonprofits need your help. Some have local chapters and in-person volunteer opportunities. Others offer ways you can help and take action from home, including by computer. You can volunteer for individual events or on an ongoing basis. Visit their websites to learn more. Check with your school counselor, local community center, church, and friends to learn about other opportunities. Invite your friends to volunteer with you!

Whether your skills and expertise include writing, fundraising, sales, graphic design, social media, website development, or other valuable skills, your help is needed.

One of the easiest ways to help is to simply share the organization's contact information and issues on your social media sites. It increases visibility of the cause and attracts future volunteers and donors.

MY STORY

I used to volunteer at a local animal shelter walking dogs. Life at an animal shelter can be devastating to an animal used to living in a loving home. Often I would be in the back of the shelter, bringing a dog in or taking another one out.

There'd be people back in the shelter looking for animals, but because they were not being assisted, many were getting ready to leave without adopting a pet. I'd jump in, engage them, and guide them to the proper animal. About 70 percent of them would end up adopting a new friend.

Your must-know people skills will also make you an effective volunteer!

Why Volunteer?

- **Volunteering makes you happier and healthier.** It's fun! Helping others is rewarding. It's a terrific way to meet new friends and contacts.

- **Volunteering helps you gain experience and get a job.** Make sure it shows up on your resume! 42% of people responsible for hiring workers consider volunteer work equal to full-time work experience. One out of every five managers responsible for hiring in the U.S. hired a candidate because of their volunteer experience. Or as in my case, volunteering can lead to a paid job with a nonprofit organization.

• **Volunteering improves your chances of getting into college or receiving a scholarship.** College admissions officers value your community service hours and long-term commitment to a cause.

 WIRED TIP: Visit www.VolunteerMatch.org or www.DoSomething.org to find volunteer opportunities.

Visit www.CharityNavigator.org or www.GuideStar.org to evaluate nonprofit organizations and to ensure they are legitimate.

We make a living by what we get, but we make a life by what we give.
—WINSTON CHURCHILL, FORMER PRIME MINISTER OF THE UK

Enthusiasm
attracts
donors.

OVERCOME THE FEAR OF FUNDRAISING

It's common for people to be afraid to ask for donations, but your current fundraising experiences (sports team, class trip, scout troop, or school band) can be used effectively for other good causes.

These tips will help you overcome any fear of fundraising for a nonprofit organization:

- Volunteer for causes you are **passionate** about.
- Think of fundraising as **helping people invest in organizations and causes they care about.** You are helping a worthy cause succeed in its mission.
- Most people are happy to make a donation. It makes them feel good to know they are helping others.

WOULD YOU LIKE TO JOIN?

Years ago, I was working at an annual weekend fly fishing show. I was fundraising for a land conservancy in northern Michigan. The group had tried to raise money and recruit new members at this show before. They had never received a single donation or new member.

First thing Saturday morning a man walked up to our table. I spoke with him about our mission of protecting land in northern Michigan. He asked me the cost of membership. I told him it was $30. He turned away. I thought to myself, "This must be what happens all the time. This is why they haven't received any donations—they've never asked!" I decided to use the show as a test to see if asking for the donation would make a difference.

As the man started to walk away, I politely called out, "Would you like to join?" He turned around immediately, pulled out his wallet, and handed me his credit card—just like that! He went on to become an annual donor. He increased his gift each year. That weekend I received a total of 16 donations from new members, about one an hour, just by asking.

 WIRED TIP: Research the website and social media sites of the organization for which you are fundraising beforehand to learn about the group's mission and programs. This will increase your confidence when asking for donations, and improve your results!

You must do the thing you think you cannot do.
—ELEANOR ROOSEVELT, FORMER FIRST LADY

Every donation advances your cause.

ASK FOR THE DONATION— THEN STOP TALKING

Once you've explained the purpose of your fundraiser and answered any questions, ask for the donation. Then be quiet. Don't utter a sound.

WHAT IT SOUNDS LIKE: ASK FOR THE DONATION

You: "I'm selling this popcorn to support our school band. Would you like to purchase some?"

Then be quiet.

Customer: *(Silence for a few seconds as he or she thinks about it...)* "How much is it?"
You: "$10.00. How many would you like to buy?"

Then BE QUIET.

Customer: "Two bags. Here's $20.00."

ANOTHER EXAMPLE

You: "We are raising money for the local food bank to help feed people in our community. Our goal is to provide 600 meals this month. Would you like to donate?"

Then be quiet.

Customer: *(Silence for a few seconds as he or she thinks about it...)* "Is my donation tax-deductible?"
You: "Yes. We will provide you with a receipt. How much would you like to donate?"

Then BE QUIET.

Customer: "Great. I'll donate $20.00."

 **WIRED TIP:** For fundraising tips visit www.SmileforTeens.com and click on "Free."

You miss 100% of the shots you don't take.
—WAYNE GRETZKY, HOCKEY LEGEND

Put your free time to work by giving it to others. You'll feel the awesome satisfaction of time and effort well spent.

ROCK THE WORLD— FIND YOUR CAUSE

HELP PEOPLE

Habitat for Humanity
www.Habitat.org
Builds and repairs houses all over the world using volunteer labor and donations.

Feeding America
www.FeedingAmerica.org
Feeding America's hungry through a nationwide network of member food banks.

Meals on Wheels
www.mowaa.org
Provides home-delivered meals to people in need.
Focuses on seniors.

National Coalition for the Homeless
www.NationalHomeless.org
Works to prevent and end homelessness.

Red Cross
www.RedCross.org
Provides disaster relief at home and abroad, CPR
certification and first-aid courses, blood donation,
and emergency preparedness.

**Never doubt that a small group of thoughtful,
committed citizens can change the world; indeed,
it's the only thing that ever has.**
—MARGARET MEAD, AMERICAN CULTURAL
ANTHROPOLOGIST AND AUTHOR

Did you know? Many reasons dogs and cats are in shelters have nothing to do with the pets themselves. Their owners may be moving somewhere that doesn't allow pets, are no longer able to afford the pet, or don't have time to take care of it.

HELP ANIMALS

Animals Asia
www.AnimalsAsia.org
Ending cruelty and restoring respect for animals.
Focuses on three major programs: Ending Bear Bile
Farming, Cat and Dog Welfare, and Zoos and
Safari Parks.

Stop Circus Suffering
www.StopCircusSuffering.com
Stop Circus Suffering is a major campaign by Animal
Defenders International (www.ad-international.org) to
end the suffering of animals in circuses.

International Anti-Poaching Foundation
www.IAPF.org
Founded by a former Australian Special Operations
soldier, IAPF applies combat skills to the war against
poaching to save endangered wildlife, including rhinos,
elephants, and tigers.

PetFinder.com

www.PetFinder.com

Help animals find their forever home. Adopt your
next best friend!

World Society for the Protection of Animals

www.wspa-international.org

Tackling animal cruelty across the globe.

 WIRED TIP: Walking dogs in animal shelters is a great
way to donate your time and give the dogs much-
needed exercise. And you get exercise too! Search
online to locate your local animal shelter.

 BONUS WIRED TIP: Looking to adopt a new puppy or
dog? Learn about how to adopt one that suits your
lifestyle at www.SmileforTeens.com and click on "FREE."

Be the change you want to see in the world.

—MAHATMA GANDHI, PRIMARY LEADER OF
INDIA'S INDEPENDENCE MOVEMENT

There can be no greater issue than
that of conservation in this country.
—Theodore Roosevelt

PROTECT OUR ENVIRONMENT

American Rivers
www.AmericanRivers.org
Protects wild rivers and conserves clean water
for people and nature.

Conservation International
www.Conservation.org
Working to ensure a healthy, productive planet
for everyone.

Land Trust Alliance
www.LandTrustAlliance.org
Promotes voluntary land conservation to save
the places people love.

National Wildlife Federation

www.NWF.org

Safeguarding America's wildlife and wild places and inspiring the future generation of conservationists.

The Nature Conservancy

www.Nature.org

Protecting ecologically important lands and waters for nature and people.

 WIRED TIP: See cool ideas about how to save land for people and wildlife and protect water quality, while accommodating growth and development: Type "conservation subdivisions" into a search engine.

Each person must live their life as a model for others.

—ROSA PARKS, CIVIL RIGHTS ACTIVIST

PUTTING IT ALL TOGETHER

We've covered a lot of territory in this book. From developing great people skills to learning how to find a job, from mastering customer service and sales techniques to preparing yourself to be an expert fundraiser and volunteer, you now have the tools to succeed.

A SMILE will set you on a path that leads to a successful, purposeful, and fulfilling life.

Always remember: **Smiles can be magical.**

NEXT STEPS

To learn more, visit the *Smile* website at:
www.SmileforTeens.com

NOTES

Introduction

2 Employers everywhere are saying. Laura Paul, "Break Poor Communication Habits," Disneyfamily.com, http://family.go.com/parenting/pkg-teen/article-774158-break-poor-communication-patterns-t/ (accessed March 2, 2014).

3 Developing face-to-face communication skills. Dan Schawbel, "Somebody's Gotta Get Hired, Right? 6 Tips to Help New Grads Land Job Offers," TIME.com, May 15, 2012, http://business.time.com/2012/05/15/somebodys-gotta-get-hired-right-6-tips-to-help-new-grads-land-job-offers/ (accessed March 2, 2014).

Chapter 1: The Top Ten People Skills

8 First impressions occur. Malcolm Gladwell, Interview with Allan Gregg, "Allan Gregg: Malcolm Gladwell-Blink-Full Show," TVO.org, November 5, 2010, www.tvo.org/video/163858/mal colm-gladwell-blink-full-show, (accessed March 2, 2014).

8 Smile and the world smiles with you. Anonymous quote made famous with lyrics written and sung by Louis Armstrong in the song, "When You're Smiling". Oprah.com, www.oprah.com/spirit/The-Power-of-a-Smile/ (accessed March 2, 2014).

11 The most positive conversations happen. Ed Keller and Brad Fay, "Facebook Can't Replace Face-to-Face Conversation," USATODAY.com, April 29, 2012, Ed Keller and Brad Fay, http://usatoday30.usatoday.com/news/opinion/forum/story/2012-04-29/facebook-face-to-face/54629816/1 (accessed March 2, 2014).

14 College admissions officers will review. Linsey Davis, Sarah Netter, Alexandra Ludka, "How to Use Social Media to Get into College," abcnews.com,

October 19, 2012, http://abcnews.go.com/Technology/social-media-hurt-college-bid/story?id=17520370 (accessed March 2, 2104).

18 Students with high scoring handshakes.
Anthony Balderrama, "Why You Need a Good Handshake," careerbuilder.com, www.careerbuilder.com/Article/CB-884-Getting-Hired-Why-You-Need-a-Good-Handshake/ (accessed March 2, 2014).

20 Friendship is an undervalued resource.
Tara Parker-Pope, "What Are Friends For? A Longer Life," NYTimes.com, April 20, 2009, www.nytimes.com/2009/04/21/health/21well.html?_r=1& (accessed March 2, 2014).

23 Multiple studies indicate that listening. Goldin Leadership Group, "Is Anybody Listening?," thecoachingcompass.com, May 25th, 2010, http://thecoachingcompass.com/tag/listening-statistics, (accessed March 2, 2014).

Chapter 2: Get That Job

32 Students are more likely to graduate. Mike Fritz, "After-School Jobs Spark Academic Success," PBS.org, December 27, 2012, www.pbs.org/newshour/updates/education/july-dec12/student_jobs.html (accessed March 2, 2014).

42 The most common mistake new employees make.
Scott Reeves, "Dress for Success," Forbes.com, April 12, 2006, www.forbes.com/2006/04/11/office-dress-codes-cx_sr_0411officedress.html (accessed March 2, 2014).

44 49% of teens report. Christine Berry, "Statistics on Teen-Stress," parentingteens.com, March 15, 2013, www.parentingteens.com/statistics-on-teen-stress/ (accessed March 2, 2014).

44 Overcome stress to be your. Sharon Jayson, "Teens and Stress: Bad Habits Begin Early," USATODAY.com, February 11, 2014, www.usatoday.com/story/news/nation/2014/02/11/stress-teens-psychological/5266739/ (accessed March 2, 2014).

Chapter 3: Keep Them Smiling

52 When you are well prepared. Steve Timmerman, "The Importance of Being Prepared," mckinleyconsulting.com, August 19, 2013, http://mckinleyconsulting.com/blog/impor tance-prepared (accessed March 2, 2014).

59 A properly written email. Lindsay Silberman, "25 Tips for Perfecting Your E-mail Etiquette," Inc.com, www.inc.com/guides/2010/06/email-etiquette.html (accessed March 2, 2014.)

62 Americans tell an average of 15 other people about. American Express® Global Customer Service Barometer, AmericanExpress.com, http://about.americanexpress.com/news/pr/2012/gcsb.aspx (accessed March 2, 2014)

64 Do not allow an unanswered message to remain. Elizabeth Anne Winters, "Top 10 Electronic Etiquette Faux Pas," Nov 11, 2010, Forbes.com, www.forbes.com/2010/11/11/tech nology-electronic-etiquette-forbes-woman-leadership-social-media.html (accessed March 2, 2014).

64 Social media requires. Jay Baer, "42 Percent of Consumers Complaining in Social Media Expect 60 Minute Response Time," convinceandconvert.com, www.convinceandconvert.com/the-social-habit/42-percent-of-consumers-complaining-in-social-media-expect-60-minute-response-time/ (accessed March 2, 2014).

Chapter 4: Treat People How You Want to be Treated

69 Seventy percent of small business. Small Business Administration, "SBA Study Determines Why Customers Leave," nbnnews.com, www.nbnnews.com/NBN/issues/2005-01-10/Business+Management/2.html (accessed March 2, 2014).

70 Two thirds of customers have walked. "What's Wrong with Customer Service?", ConsumerReports.org, July, 2011, www.consumerreports.org/cro/magazine-archive/2011/july/shopping/customer-service/overview/index.htm (accessed March 2, 2014).

72 70% of how you're perceived on the phone. Lydia Ramsey, "Making The Most of First Impressions," mannersthatsell.com, http://mannersthatsell.com/businessimpressions/ (accessed March 2, 2014).

Chapter 5: Sell More with Great People Skills

82 The best salespeople are. Steve W. Martin, "Seven Personality Traits of Top Salespeople," HBR.org, June 27, 2011, http://blogs.hbr.org/cs/2011/06/the_seven_personality_traits_o.html (accessed March 2, 2014).

84 It is estimated that $83 billion is lost. The Cost of Poor Customer Service: The Economic Impact of the Customer Experience in the U.S. (Genesys, October, 2009), (accessed March 2, 2014).

Chapter 6: Keep Customers Smiling After the Sale

96 It takes 12 positive customer service experiences.
"Customer Service Facts," customerservicemanager.com, www.customerservicemanager.com/customer-service-facts.htm (accessed March 2, 2014).

97 Satisfied customers who have problems resolved.
James Digby, White House Office of Consumer Affairs, "50 Facts About Customer Experience," returnonbehavior.com, http://returnonbehavior.com/2010/10/50-facts-about-customer-expe rience-for-2011/ (accessed March 2, 2014).

98 80% of companies think they're providing superior service. James Allen, Frederick F. Reicheld, Barney Hamilton, and Rob Markey, "Closing the Delivery Gap: How to Achieve True Customer-Led Growth," Bain.com, 2005, www.bain.com/bainweb/pdfs/cms/hotTopics/closingdeliver gap.pdf, 1. (accessed March 2, 2014).

Chapter 7: Be a Rock Star

103 There'd be people back in the shelter. "Going the Extra Smile," AnimalSheltering.org, January/February 2014, www.animalsheltering.org/resources/magazine/jan-feb-2014/Going-the-Extra-Smile.pdf (accessed March 2, 2014).

103 Volunteering makes you happier and healthier. Gretchen Rubin, "Volunteer. Give Pro Bono. Help Others. It's the Right Thing to Do, and It Will Boost Your Happiness," Forbes.com, April 16, 2011, www.forbes.com/sites/gretchenrubin/2011/04/16/volunteer-give-pro-bono-help-others-its-the-right-thing-to-do-and-it-will-boost-your-happiness/ (accessed March 2, 2014).

103 **Volunteering helps you gain job experience
and get a job.** Reid Hoffman, "The LinkedIn Volunteer
Marketplace: Connecting Professionals to Non-Profit
Volunteer Opportunities," January 15, 2014, blog.LinkedIn.com,
http://blog.linkedin.com/2014/01/15/the-linkedin-volunteer-
marketplace-connecting-professionals-to-nonprofit-volunteer-
opportunities/ (accessed March 2, 2014).

104 **Volunteering improves your chances.** Miriam Salpeter,
"Community Service Work Increasingly Important for College
Applicants," Money.USNews.com, http://money.usnews.com/
money/blogs/outside-voices-careers/2011/11/30/community
service-work-increasingly-important-for-college-applicants
(accessed March 2, 2014).

107 **"Why did you give?"** This is a famous fundraising saying.

112 **Did you know? Many reasons dogs and cats are in
shelters have nothing to do with.** Jane Harrell, "Six Common
Misconceptions About Pet Adoption," Petfinder.com, www.pet
finder.com/pet-adoption/pet-adoption-information/misconcep
tions-pet-adoption/ (accessed March 2, 2014).

INDEX

ABOUT THE AUTHOR

KIRT MANECKE is an award-winning author and a sales, marketing, fundraising, and business development specialist with over 30 years of experience making customers smile. A proven "natural" salesman, Kirt helps companies build lasting, profitable relationships with clients through strategic marketing and expert customer service.

As founder and former owner of an award-winning specialty retail business in Michigan, Kirt created and implemented an innovative six-week training program that maximized customer satisfaction and sales by teaching employees many of the skills presented in his award-winning first book, *Smile: Sell More with Amazing Customer Service*. Many of these skills have been customized for teens and included in *Smile & Succeed for Teens*.

In his free time, Kirt volunteers his skills to help end animal cruelty and preserve natural spaces in the United States and abroad. Kirt is founder and chair of the Michigan chapter of Animals Asia, a group devoted to rescuing animals from cruelty, raising awareness, and improving public policy affecting animals. Kirt lives with his rescue dog Ozzie in Milford, Michigan.

Learn more about Kirt at www.SmiletheBook.com and www.SmileforTeens.com.

Smile: Sell More with Amazing Customer Service

CREATE PROFITABLE, LIFELONG CUSTOMERS IN 60 MINUTES OR LESS!

You may also want to read Kirt's first book, *Smile: Sell More with Amazing Customer Service*. Winner of 8 awards, *Smile* has been featured in *STORES* magazine, published by the National Retail Federation, *Animal Sheltering Magazine* from The Humane Society, *The Old Schoolhouse Magazine*, and *American Salon,* among many others.

Smile is a 60-minute crash course in customer service and sales. Packed with indispensable tips, proven techniques, and "must-do-now" strategies for delighting customers, *Smile* makes customer service and sales intuitive and fun.

IN *SMILE*, YOU WILL DISCOVER HOW TO:

- Train others quickly and easily in **friendly** customer service and sales
- Put more money into your wallet, starting today, with excellent customer service
- Increase sales, repeat business, and positive buzz about YOU, starting TODAY

- Boost your sales and service confidence
- ASK for the sale or donation—and get it!
- Handle customer objections and complaints effectively
- Increase your sales through suggestive selling

It's all a quick, 60-minute (or less) read away. Destined to become a classic, this indispensable guide will help you surprise and delight your customers and sell more. Whether you're an employer or an employee, a workplace veteran or the latest hire, the approach is the same: make them SMILE—and watch success and record sales follow!

"An excellent crash course in customer service—read it and become a quick study at delighting those you serve!"
—KATYA ANDRESEN, AUTHOR OF
ROBIN HOOD MARKETING

"Customer service is the heart of all business—get it right and experience success or settle on being mediocre. This book helps you get it right!"
—ROBERT LAMEIER, PRESIDENT AND CEO,
MIAMI SAVINGS BANK

"Manecke reminds us that these simple manners are essential to any company's bottom line and shows how to implement them in a purposeful, effective way." Star Rating: 5 out of 5.
—SAN FRANCISCO BOOK REVIEW

**Learn more at
www.SmileforTeens.com
and
www.SmiletheBook.com**